How to Make a Log Cabin Quilt Block

MW00633506

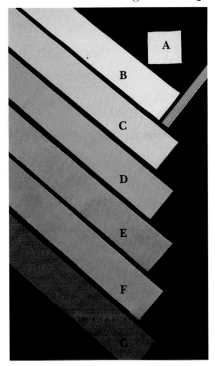

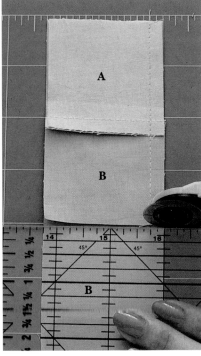

1) Cut one scant 2¼" (6 cm) square from Fabric A. Cut one scant 2¼" (6 cm) strip (page 3) from each of six different fabrics. Label strips from B to G, as shown.

2) Place solid square on Strip B, right sides together. Stitch along one side. Trim strip even with square. Press seam allowance away from center square.

3) Place pieced unit on remaining length of Strip B, as shown. Stitch on long side. Trim strip even with bottom of pieced unit. Press seam allowance away from center square.

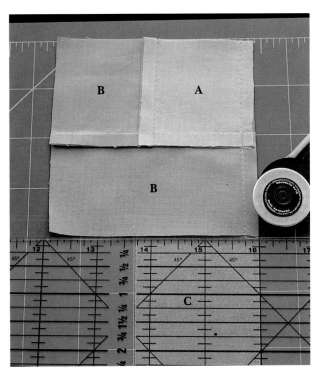

4) Place three-piece unit on Strip C at 90° angle to most recent seam. Stitch on long side. Trim strip even with bottom of pieced unit. Press seam allowance away from center square.

5) Place four-piece unit on remaining length of Strip C at 90° angle to most recent seam. Continue in this manner, stitching two strips of each color to pieced unit in sequence. Press seam allowances away from center square.

Basic Piecing Techniques

Cutting the pieces for the Log Cabin block is simple to do using a rotary cutter and 24"-long (61 cm) see-through ruler. Piecing is the same for most patchwork, and machine setup and pressing are the same also. Accuracy is critical to successful piecing. A small error can multiply itself many times, resulting in a block or a quilt that does not fit together properly. Check the accuracy of your cutting and stitching frequently. You may want to practice the cutting and stitching techniques on a small project before using them on a large project.

Cutting Techniques

The quick cutting techniques that follow are both timesaving and accurate. Instead of cutting each piece of the quilt individually, stack several layers of fabric and cut them into crosswise strips. The pieces are then cut from these strips, eliminating the need for templates. Tape three or four thin strips of fine sandpaper across the width of the bottom of a see-through ruler, using double-stick tape. This prevents the ruler from slipping when you are cutting fabric. Determine the grainline by folding the fabric in half and holding it by the selvages. Then shift one side until the fabric hangs straight. It is not necessary to straighten quilting fabrics that are off-grain or to pull threads or tear fabrics to find the grainline.

Good-quality cutting equipment helps ensure that every piece you cut is exactly the right size and that all the pieces fit together perfectly. Use a rotary cutter with a sharp blade and a cutting mat with a printed grid.

How to Cut Fabric Strips

1) **Lay** fabric on cutting mat, with fold along a grid line. Place ruler on fabric close to raw edge, at 90° angle to fold. Trim along edge of ruler, taking care not to move fabric. Hold ruler firmly; apply steady, firm pressure on blade. Stop when rotary cutter gets past hand. Leave blade in position; reposition hand ahead of blade. Hold firmly and continue cutting. Make sure the fabric and ruler do not shift position.

2) **Place** ruler on fabric, aligning trimmed edge with appropriate measurement on ruler. Hold ruler firmly; cut as in step 1. After cutting several strips, check fabric to be sure it is still on-grain.

Stitching & Pressing Techniques

As in most piecing, ¼" (6 mm) seam allowances are used in Log Cabin blocks. Check your machine and presser feet to determine the most accurate way of sewing a perfect ¼" (6 mm) seam, or place a piece of tape on your machine bed where the edge of the fabric should line up. Use a stitch length of 12 or 15 stitches per inch (2.5 cm) and make sure tension is even so that the stitches will not ravel when small pieced units are handled and pressed. Press using steam rather than pressure, to prevent the layers from imprinting on the right side. Press the seam allowances first from the wrong side; then press them again lightly from the right side.

Borders

A border frames the quilt and visually finishes the edges. The three basic styles of borders are lapped borders, borders with interrupted corners, and mitered borders. In general, a lapped border is used with solid fabrics or all-over prints, and a mitered border is used with striped or border-print fabrics. A border with interrupted corners is suitable with all types of fabrics.

The border strips are cut after the quilt top is pieced and measured, because even the slightest variance in seam allowances can affect the finished size of the quilt top. The cut length of the border strips is determined by measuring through the middle of the quilt; this maintains the overall dimensions.

Border strips are usually cut on the crosswise grain and pieced together for the necessary length. If seaming is required, the seam placement may be random; however, the seams should generally not be closer than 12" (30.5 cm) to a corner. For less noticeable seams, piece the strips diagonally. Borders cut from striped fabrics or border prints will usually have to be cut on the lengthwise grainline. For a double border, apply inner border, following steps 1 and 2. Measure the quilt top across and down the middle, including the inner border; cut and apply the outer border as for inner border.

How to Make and Apply a Lapped Border

Single border. 1) Measure the quilt top across the middle. Cut two strips equal to this measurement, piecing as necessary; width of strips is equal to finished width of border plus ½" (1.3 cm).

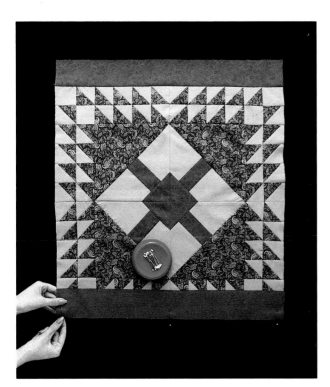

2) Pin strip to upper edge of quilt top at center and ends, right sides together; pin along length, easing in any fullness. Stitch; press seam allowances toward border. Repeat at lower edge.

3) Measure quilt top down the middle, including border strips. Cut two strips as in step 1. Pin and stitch strips to sides of quilt top as in step 2. Press seam allowances toward border.

Layering & Basting a Quilt

After the quilt top is completed, the backing and the batting are cut, and the three layers are basted together. The backing and batting should extend 2" to 4" (5 to 10 cm) beyond the edges on all sides. Basting keeps the layers from shifting. Quilts can be basted using a needle and thread or rustproof safety pins. If basting with thread, use white cotton thread and a large milliners or darning needle. Use a running stitch about 1" (2.5 cm) long.

How to Layer and Baste a Quilt

1) **Mark** the center of each side of the quilt top at raw edges with safety pins; repeat for batting and backing. Tape backing, wrong side up, on the work surface; work from center to corners on each side, stretching fabric slightly.

2) **Place** batting over the backing, matching pins. Smooth, but do not stretch, working from center to sides. Place quilt top right side up over batting, matching the pins; smooth, but do not stretch.

3) **Baste** from the center of quilt to pins on sides; if thread-basting, pull stitches snug so layers will not shift, and backstitch at the ends. Avoid basting on the marked quilting lines or through the seams. (Both basting methods are shown.)

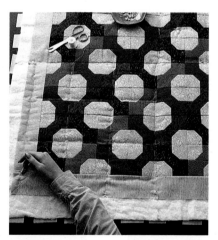

4) **Baste** one quarter-section in parallel rows about 6" (15 cm) apart, working toward the raw edges. If thread-basting, also baste quarter-section in parallel rows in opposite direction. Repeat for all quarter-sections.

5) **Remove** the tape from backing. Fold edges of backing over batting and edges of quilt top, to prevent raw edges of fabric from raveling and to prevent the batting from catching on the needle and feed dogs during quilting. Pin-baste.

Machine-guided Quilting Techniques

Set up the sewing machine in an area where the quilt will be supported both to the left of and behind the machine. Do not allow the quilt to hang over the back or the side of the sewing table; this will cause the quilt to feed through the machine unevenly, resulting in an uneven stitch length.

For machine-guided quilting, attach an Even Feed™ foot, or walking foot, if one is available; this type of presser foot helps to prevent puckering. Use a stitch length of 8 to 10 stitches per inch (2.5 cm).

Thread the machine with cotton or monofilament nylon thread. With either thread type, loosen the needle thread tension, if necessary, so the bobbin thread does not show on the right side. Cotton thread is traditionally used for quilting. Select the thread color according to how much you want the stitching to show. Frequently one thread color that blends with all of the fabrics in the quilt is used throughout.

Monofilament nylon thread is now popular for machine quilting, because with this thread type, it is usually not necessary to change thread colors.

Choose the clear for most fabric colors and the smoke for dark fabrics. The nylon thread is used only in the needle, and a cotton thread is used in the bobbin.

Plan the sequence of the quilting before you begin to stitch. The sequence varies according to the style of the quilt. Generally, begin anchoring the quilt horizontally and vertically by stitching in the ditch of a seamline near the center, then anchoring any borders. This prevents the layers from shifting. Next, stitch along any sashing strips or between the blocks, starting in the center and working toward the sides. Once the quilt has been anchored into sections, quilt the areas within the blocks and borders.

Stitch continuously, with as few starts and stops as possible. Position your hands on either side of the presser foot. Gently press down and hold the fabric taut to prevent the layer from shifting, which would cause puckers or tucks. Ease any excess fabric under the presser foot as you stitch. If a tuck does occur, release the stitches for 3" (7.5 cm) or more, and restitch, easing in excess fabric.

How to Quilt Using Machine-guided Techniques

Stitch-in-the-ditch quilting. Stitch over the seamline, stitching in the well of the seam.

Outline quilting. Stitch about ¼" (6 mm) from seamline, starting at the corner.

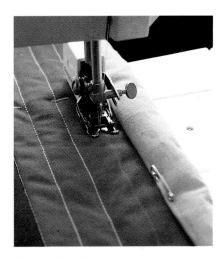

Channel quilting. Stitch on marked quilting lines, starting with inner line and working toward edge.

How to Quilt a Basic Project

1) Roll one or both sides of quilt to within 3" (7.5 cm) of the first vertical quilting line to be stitched; this is usually a seamline near the center. Secure the roll with bicycle pants clips or large safety pins. Hold quilt over shoulder or in lap. Stitch along quilting lines; allow quilt to feed evenly into the machine. Secure thread tails. Reroll quilt as necessary.

How to Secure Thread Tails

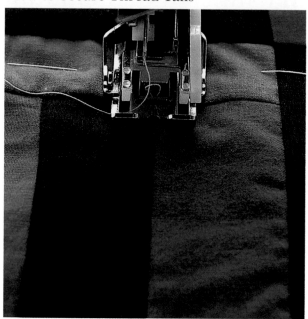

1) Draw up the bobbin thread to the quilt top, by turning flywheel by hand and stopping with needle at highest position. Pull needle thread to bring bobbin thread up through the fabric. Stitch several short stitches to secure the threads at the beginning of stitching line, gradually increasing the stitch length for about ½" (1.3 cm), to desired length. Reverse procedure at end of stitching.

Binding Techniques

Double binding, which is cut on the straight of grain, provides a durable finished edge for a quilt. It can be cut to match the border or cut from a coordinating or contrasting fabric.

How to Bind a Quilt

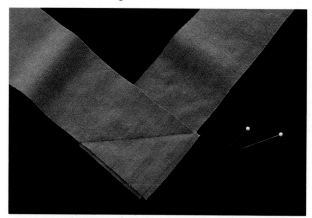

1) Cut strips on crosswise grain 2½" (6.5 cm) wide for binding. Pin strips, right sides together, at right angles, if it is necessary to piece strips. Stitch diagonally across strips. Trim seam allowances to ¼" (6 mm). Press seam open. Trim point. Press binding strip in half lengthwise, wrong sides together.

2) Place binding strip on upper edge of the quilt top, matching raw edges. Trim the binding to extend 1" (2.5 cm) beyond the quilt top at each end. Pin along length, easing in any fullness.

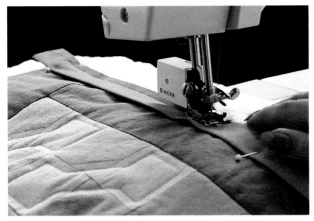

3) Stitch binding strip to quilt, a scant ¼" (6 mm) from the raw edges of binding. Trim excess batting and backing to a scant ½" (1.3 cm) from stitching for binding.

4) Wrap binding strip snugly around edge of quilt, covering stitching line on back of quilt; pin in the ditch of the seam.

5) Stitch in the ditch on right side of quilt, catching binding on back of quilt; for less noticeable stitches, use monofilament nylon thread in the needle.

6) Repeat steps 2 to 4 for lower edge of quilt. Trim ends of upper and lower binding strips even with edges of quilt top.

7) Repeat steps 2 and 3 for sides of quilt. Trim ends of binding strips to extend ½" (1.3 cm) beyond the finished edges of the quilt.

8) Fold binding along the stitching line. Fold ½" (1.3 cm) end of binding over finished edge; press in place. Wrap binding around edge and stitch in the ditch as in steps 4 and 5. Slipstitch end.

GALLERY OF LOG CABIN QUILTS

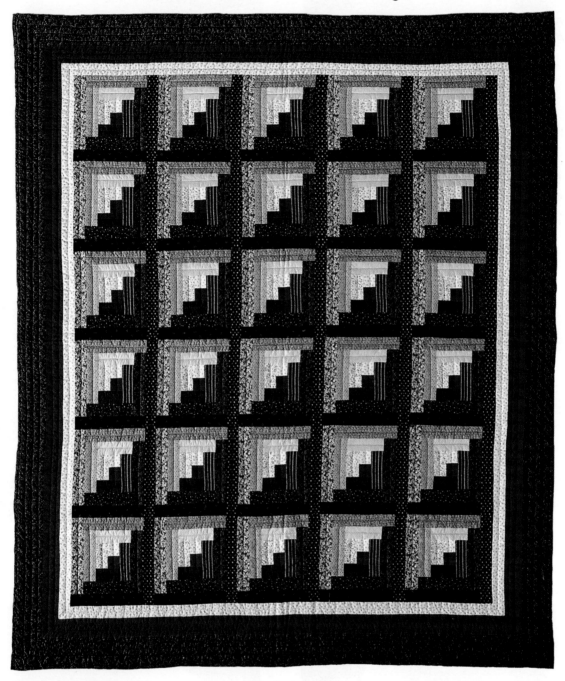

Finished size: 89" × 102"   **Block size:** 12"   **Block arrangement:** Plain

A favorite log cabin getaway, built in the 1930s, was the inspiration for this "Log Cabin for the Log Cabin" quilt, which suggests the white chinking in the walls, brown logs, and warmth coming from the stone fireplace. The quilt decorates a four-poster bed and is the maker's first quilt. Done in warm colors, the blocks are everyone's image of the traditional Log Cabin design, with strong centers and sharp light-and-dark contrast. The borders frame the blocks well and act as an attractive drop on the sides of the bed. This quilt can be an inspiration for anyone wishing to make a wonderful bedcover for their own home and wanting to start with a simple but beautiful design.

Made by: Marge Herrington, New Brighton, MN

Finished size: 72" × 86"   **Block size:** 14"   **Block arrangement:** Plain

The Octagon House Museum rightly showcases this quilt in its parlour, which is decorated very elegantly with mid-Victorian furnishings. The house, an eight-sided building, was constructed in 1855 for a judge and his family. It has been a museum since 1964. The quilt was made in the 1870s by "Abigail Page Bailey, first white child born in Hudson." It features a mixture of many fabrics, textures, colors, and patterns. The wonderful red squares in the centers of the blocks are embroidered with different flowers, making the quilt a relative of the Victorian silk-embroidered crazy quilts of the era. When new, it would probably have been used as a decorative piece on a fancy love seat. Today, it serves as a valuable inventory of the fabrics in use at the time of its origin.

Owned by: Octagon House Museum, Hudson, WI

Finished size: 66" × 88"   **Block size:** 11"   **Block arrangement:** Barn raising

This example of the "barn raising" arrangement of Log Cabin blocks was purchased in Maine and probably was made between 1900 and 1920. The maker of this quilt obviously decided to make a bold statement with her color selection, staying with only four colors and using them in a very particular way. The large red centers are like jewels on a necklace of sharply contrasting blue-and-yellow strips placed on a stark white background. As a bed quilt, this piece would certainly be the focal point of the room.

Owned by: Patricia Cox, Edina, MN

Finished size: 60" × 80"   **Block size:** 7½"   **Block arrangement:** Barn raising

Traditional Log Cabin blocks made from wonderful contemporary cotton prints would have made a lovely wall hanging or bed quilt all by themselves, but Jeanne Tanamachi has added star sashing between the blocks of her "Simply Colorado" quilt to add even more interest and color highlights. The sashing, made of two strips with triangles at the corners and connecting squares of the star color, consists of fabrics that blend in with the blocks so the overall "barn raising" arrangement of the blocks is not disturbed.

Made by: Jeanne Tanamachi, Lauderdale, MN

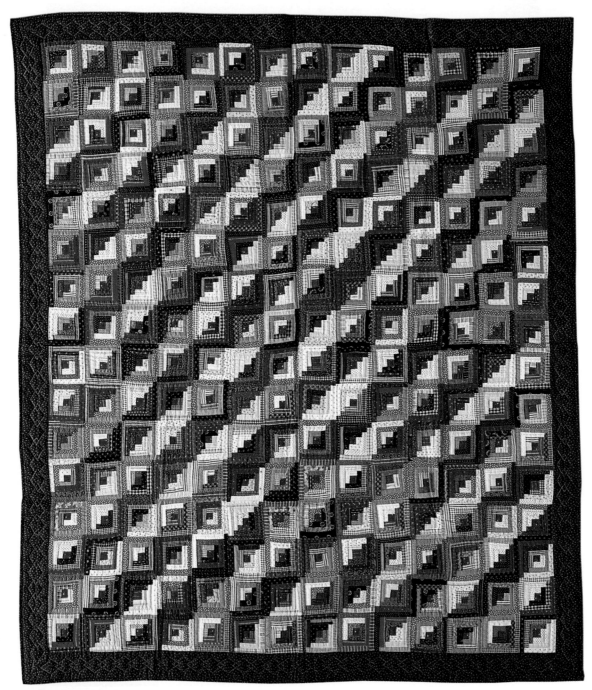

Finished size: 74" × 84"   **Block size:** 5"   **Block arrangement:** Straight furrows

This quilt began as a mint-condition antique quilt top, found in Ohio, and probably was made around 1890. The borders and quilting were added recently. The wonderful prints and plaids were most likely pulled from the scrap bag of a busy home sewer, and give the quilt a very cheerful quality. The dark and light values are very distinct and are arranged diagonally into a "straight furrows" pattern, reminiscent of the plowed fields of the American farm. Notice that one block is turned the wrong way—this was often done in old quilts in order to show humility, "because only God can make something perfect."

Owned by: Patricia Cox, Edina, MN

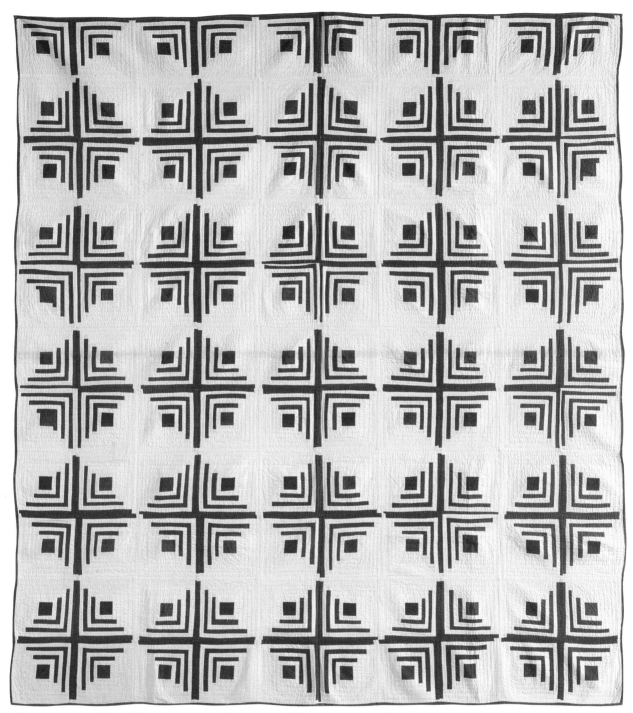

Finished size: 72" × 78"   **Block size:** 7½"   **Block arrangement:** Sunshine and shadows

This delightful "sunshine and shadows" Log Cabin quilt was probably made around 1915, but has very contemporary appeal. The red-and-white color combination, always a favorite with quiltmakers and quilt collectors, is used in a unique way. One half of each block is left entirely white, and the other half uses a red strip for every other row only. The effect is graphic, light, and cheerful. A quilt with only two colors may indicate that the quiltmaker had access to new fabric yardage and wasn't confined to using scraps, or that her design sense favored a bold and simple look to her quilts. Notice that this quilt does not have borders, but uses an extra row of blocks at the top for a look that is different from the bottom of the quilt.

Owned by: Patricia Cox, Edina, MN

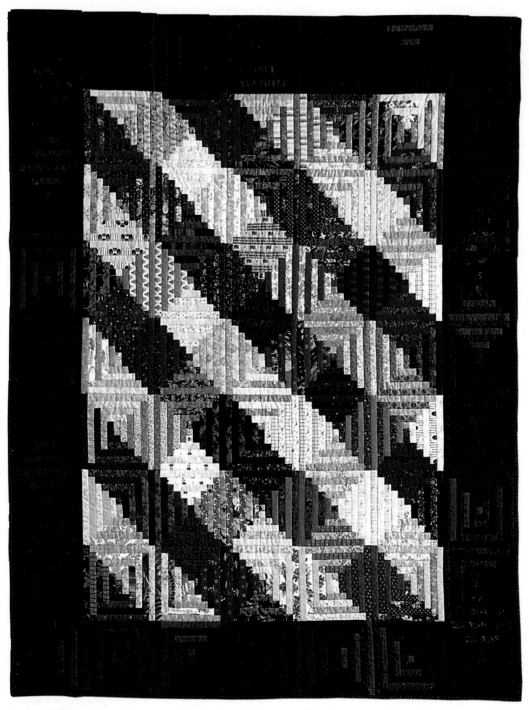

Finished size: 56" × 72"   **Block size:** 8¼"   **Block arrangement:** Courthouse steps

This contemporary Log Cabin quilt contains many interesting print fabrics and a dynamic color scheme. Each block builds out from the center square in a one-side-to-opposite-side manner, with each of the four sides consisting of only two alternating fabrics. This means that each block is different from every other block in the quilt. The overall arrangement of the color values resembles the "straight furrows" arrangement of the more traditional Log Cabin pattern. The border continues the same block pattern in very dark color values for an effect that is fascinating, especially when the piece is used as a wall hanging.

Made by: Jeanne Tanamachi, Lauderdale, MN

Finished size: 50" square   **Block size:** 8¼"   **Block arrangement:** Courthouse steps

Another contemporary "courthouse steps" variation of the Log Cabin design plays with color-value and transparency effects, inviting the eye to wander the surface and discover the various design elements of this quilt. Each side of the block, made up of simple two-color combinations with slight value differences, is juxtaposed against the three other sides. Each block is also split into parts of a secondary design of color values that darken as they approach the border. And the border itself emphasizes the color-value diagonals set up in the blocks, framing this surprisingly subtle, yet very decorative, wall hanging.

Made by: Jeanne Tanamachi, Lauderdale, MN

Finished size: 58" × 80"   **Block size:** 10"   **Block arrangement:** Plain

"School's Out" is a contemporary treatment of a traditional Log Cabin design, an aptly named quilt that has real eye appeal. The different shades of blue are a perfect "water" background for fish cut from print fabrics and appliquéd onto the quilt top. The effect is very natural, with fish swimming over block boundaries and into the border. The simplicity of the Log Cabin pattern, the graphic quality of the design, and the color gradation that suggests light filtering into the water all combine to create an exciting underwater world.

Made by: Jean Kempfer, Margate, FL

Owned by: Gene Everson, Louisville, KY